WHO INVENTED
LEMONADE?

WHO INVENTED LEMONADE?

THE POWER OF POSITIVE PERSPECTIVE

Joshua Shaw
and
Alexandra Barzvi, Ph.D.

Foreword by Donald J. Trump

iUniverse, Inc.
New York Lincoln Shanghai

WHO INVENTED LEMONADE?
THE POWER OF POSITIVE PERSPECTIVE

iUniverse books may be ordered through booksellers or by contacting:

iUniverse
2021 Pine Lake Road, Suite 100
Lincoln, NE 68512
www.iuniverse.com
1-800-Authors (1-800-288-4677)

ISBN-13: 978-0-595-37861-6 (pbk)
ISBN-13: 978-0-595-82234-8 (ebk)
ISBN-10: 0-595-37861-7 (pbk)
ISBN-10: 0-595-82234-7 (ebk)

Printed in the United States of America

Introduction

Who invented lemonade? The question seems so deceptively simple, who would ever think to ask it? But try to answer it and you'll find that, far from being simple, the question explores the nature of human creativity, endeavor, strength, and individual vision. What kind of person does it take to transform the sour sting of lemon juice into the sweet refreshment of lemonade? We may have been drinking it for centuries, but have we ever really stopped to consider who first saw the amazing possibilities beyond the immediate "problem" and came up with something as wonderfully simple and delicious as lemon juice mixed with sugar and water?

We've all heard the one about taking life's lemons and turning them into lemonade. In fact, we've heard it so many times that it barely means anything anymore. But by imagining the path of the first individual who literally turned lemons into lemonade, we gain valuable insights into the power of creative thinking, entrepreneurial decision making, and living a life beyond fear.

So who *did* invent lemonade? We'll posit a young boy, fuelled by curiosity about the world around him and filled with a kind of inquisitive imagination often lost prior to adulthood. Our young boy questions everything and everyone around him, peers and adults alike; his mind is agile and flexible, not rigid or conformist; he is resourceful and enterprising rather than imitative and repetitive; he acts upon his observations rather than passively accepting them. To a child with a mind like this, lemons are not an obstacle—they're a necessary and valuable ingredient for the solution. Follow this young boy's journey toward discovery, and you will learn not only the secret of who invented lemonade but how you can invent it too!

Alexandra Barzvi Ph.D

Contents

Foreword ix

My Story behind the Story xi

The Story of Who Invented Lemonade

A Great Big Lemon 1

Billy, the Prince of Lemonville 7

Taking the Leap 14

An Unexpected Blend 21

Beyond No 28

An End and a Beginning 35

Putting It All Together 41

Billy's Lemon-Aid Stand 51

About the Authors 57

And What about Autism Speaks?.................61

Smiles for the Cure 65

Foreword

By
Donald J. Trump:

Josh Shaw knows about looking for the best in any situation, about finding the recipe for success in any area of life. He's a firm believer in looking for the solution instead of dwelling on the problem, which is a wise choice. People who are looking for inspiration will find it here.

People sometimes think I have a Midas touch that turns everything I manage into a huge success. I wish. I've had to make a lot of lemonade in my time, metaphorically speaking, and it's a process no one should underestimate or undermined. I've learned a lot from making the best of not-so-great scenarios, and I have had opportunities surface that I would not have noticed before.

The very first task assignment I gave on *The Apprentice* was to sell lemonade. People associate many things with lemonade—from lemonade stands in their youth to overcoming obstacles as adults. Josh makes his story clear, accessible, and entertaining, and—like *The Apprentice*—he provides an educational subtext that will prove enlightening.

The proceeds from *Who Invented Lemonade?* will benefit Autism Speaks. This is in line with my thinking because it's good to give back, and it's not that hard to do. Neither is reading this book—so tune in, pay attention, and the so-called lemons in your life could take on a whole new perspective.

Congratulations, Josh. Nice job! Keep making lemonade!

Donald J. Trump

My Story behind the Story

I have long wanted to write this book to share the lessons I have learned in my life. My life hasn't been extraordinary—it's been a journey, filled with ups and downs, just like yours. Along this journey, though, I have developed a recipe for success that works in every area of life.

As I said, my young life has not been extraordinary—not terribly difficult, but not fantastically easy either, more like an uneven road with obstacles of varying shapes and sizes, the kinds of things that we all face in some way during our lives. What I have learned, though, and what I want to share in the story you are about to read, is that even though you can't control or anticipate all the obstacles that might fall across your path, you *always* have the power to choose *how* you are going to handle them. We all have problems, but each of us also has the ability to transform those problems into solutions, to turn lemons into lemonade—it's just a matter of choosing to do it.

Some might say I've been dealt a few lemons in life. I was raised in a small town that rivaled Pleasantville with perfect houses, gardens, marriages, families, cars, pets, and vacations. Looking back, of course, I realize that there were all sorts of problems beneath this perfect exterior, and my childhood there has become a huge source of strength to me now. However, at the age of six, when my parents became the only family in town to get divorced, it seemed like we were the only ones with a problem. In this perfect community, my parents' split branded us the "black sheep." There were strange looks, malicious rumors, pitying whispers, and feigned understanding accompanied by phony sweetness.

The stigma of being the only broken family in town was compounded by no longer having the same financial resources as everyone else. Summer jobs replaced summer camp, and vacations spent at home with one parent replaced trips to sunny Florida or Puerto Rico with both.

As if these lemons weren't big enough, on July 4 of 1989, on the day of my eldest sister's wedding, my father had a massive heart attack and died at the young age of forty-seven. For the first time since the divorce eight years earlier, our family had gathered for the wedding and had celebrated the happy occasion together with great joy. Within hours, my father, my mentor, my friend, was gone. I was only fourteen; the confusion, the sadness, the pain I felt is still difficult to describe.

Although it might seem I was handed some big disadvantages at a tender age, I have actually been supremely blessed—with passion, with a love for life, and, most importantly, with the ability to make lemonade out of even the biggest lemons.

My family, friends, and especially my wife have all helped me learn from and grow through my experiences:

From as far back as I can remember, my mother has been right behind me coaching and mentoring me with a loving and caring heart, constantly teaching me to believe in myself and my dreams. She taught me the importance of positive thinking and gave me the power and confidence to go after my dreams no matter what. She taught me to see the world as a wonderful place where I could breathe freely and paint murals as big as I wanted them. She was a constant source of wisdom, always telling me things like, "Nobody can upset you unless you allow them to," or, "You can be anything you want to be."

In a different but equally important way, my father has been an amazing source of strength for me. He was a passionate man who lived every day to its fullest, and he loved his family and friends deeply. His death was the worst thing that ever happened to me, but I now realize that through it, I learned about life; it provided me with a different understanding of reality and true happiness. My father, in life and in death, has taught me to put things into perspective, seize every day, treasure every moment, and live life to the fullest.

Last, but not least, my wife is a tremendous source of strength and happiness—she truly completes me. Her remarkable mind, even manner, genuine appreciation for love, and endless commitment to family have made my life plentiful in ways I never imagined. Most of all, her faith in me continues to fuel my passions in life and in business. She brightens my day, freshens my air, and feeds my soul. She is my one and only.

So you see, while some might say I have been unlucky or grew up as an underdog, I know I am blessed, because I have chosen to turn all my "lemons" into lemonade. The story you are about to read is about the weaknesses and strengths we all have inside of us and about the importance of choosing to make lemonade out of every single lemon that falls onto our path.

This is our story…

One

A Great Big Lemon

Billy felt different as he walked home from school that Friday. He couldn't put his finger on it, but all around him, the world seemed somehow richer, more interesting.

That afternoon in history class, they had studied the world's great inventors. Billy had learned about how Alexander Graham Bell had invented the telephone, about Edison and the light bulb, about the Wright brothers and their crazy flying machine, and, of course, about the grandfather of them all, Leonardo da Vinci, whose mixture of curiosity, fearlessness, and creativity Billy found especially exhilarating.

Until today, Billy had never even imagined that there had been a world without telephones. As he made his way home that afternoon, he realized how many things around him he had taken for granted, and he tried to imagine life before light bulbs or airplanes. He was amazed at what a difference these inventions had made to the world and wondered with excitement what kinds of inventions might change his world—maybe even in his own lifetime. He wished he could talk to his dad about it.

Billy's dad had died a few months earlier, and the pain was still fresh. He loved his mom and had plenty of good friends, but he still felt that there was something huge missing from his life—he thought about his father all the time, hoping he was watching over him from somewhere, although he didn't know much about that stuff.

As soon as he got home, Billy forced these thoughts from his mind, as he had a lot to do. Tomorrow was a big day for Billy: this was the Saturday that he was going to set up a lemonade stand for his class fundraising contest. Mrs. Carson had given the class a challenge: each student had to come up with an enterprising way to raise money for a World Hunger charity, and the student who raised the most would win the contest.

This assignment excited Billy. He liked the idea of thinking up something clever to do that would be fun but would also help feed children who didn't have as much as he did; he loved the idea of pitching in, and he wanted more than anything to win this contest. He thought about it long and hard, tossing ideas around in his head, wishing his dad were there to help him. He thought about setting up a carwash, but he was just one boy, and he didn't think he could wash very many cars in one day. He thought about having a yard sale, but he decided he didn't have enough to sell. Finally, Billy came upon an idea that seemed perfect: he would set up the best, busiest, most successful lemonade stand ever.

Billy, who lived just a few blocks from the neighborhood pool, knew that he had to wait for the right weather before he put his plan into action, and this weekend they were finally forecasting a hot, sunny day. So instead of dropping his bag in the hall and running out to play with his dog, Sam, he took out a notebook and headed to the kitchen to make preparations. All afternoon, as he picked the brightest, juiciest lemons from the batch she brought home from the grocery store and squeezed them into pitchers of juice, he kept thinking about the crowds that would surround his lemonade stand the next day and about how he would squeeze every last dime out of it, just like he was squeezing the lemons. He thought he should make a sign but didn't know what to write on it, so he decided to leave that until the morning—maybe he would have a great idea before then.

That night as Billy lay in bed waiting for his mom to come in and say goodnight, he started missing his father a lot; nighttime was especially hard for Billy, as this was when he and his dad had had their best talks. Billy would always learn so much that he'd wake up the next morning still thinking, and was always excited to face the day more knowledgeable than he had been the day before. He missed his father so much that he couldn't imagine the sadness ever going away.

When his mother came in and sat down on the edge of his bed, as she did every night, she could see that he was thinking serious thoughts.

"What's up little guy?" she asked.

"I was just thinking," he answered.

"Looks serious. I bet I can help. Are you thinking about your big day tomorrow?"

"Yeah. Well, kind of. Not exactly. I was just wondering why Dad had to die. I mean, it seems so unfair. All the other kids have dads, and I don't have one, and I just don't understand it. Why are we so unlucky?"

"Oh Billy, it's so complicated. I know how much you miss him. I miss him too—" she began.

"But we learned about all these amazing people today," Billy interrupted, "they invented all these amazing things—telephones and light bulbs—but still, the doctors couldn't save Daddy's life. Why did it have to happen to us?"

Billy's mother sighed deeply and looked into his pleading young eyes.

"There isn't a simple answer to that, sweetie. Sometimes…" She trailed off as she tried to think about all the big lessons her son was learning at such a young age.

"Maybe it'll help if I tell you a story. You're selling lemonade tomorrow, right?"

"Yeah. What does that have to do with the story?"

"Oh, but it has everything to do with the story. This is the story of young Billy the Prince, a little boy just about your age. He was the first person *ever* to make lemonade."

Although Billy knew his mother was just making it up that the prince's name so it was the same as his, he wanted to hear the story, so he asked her to continue.

Two

Billy, the Prince of Lemonville

Once upon a time there was a young prince named Billy, and he lived in the kingdom of Lemonville. Lemonville was a very unhappy place; for years, the kingdom had lived under what everyone thought of as a terrible blight— an overabundance of lemons. There were many lemon trees in the town, and every year the trees would produce more and more fruit. But the unhappy people of Lemonville considered lemons far too sour to eat, and thus useless; they spent all of their time and energy trying to get rid of the lemons that fell from the trees. They would pile them up, put them in giant crates, and wheel them out of town. They would shove them into barrels and throw them into the river. They would do anything and everything they could to get rid of the lemons.

But still they piled up, faster than anyone could cart them away, year after year, more and more lemons! Everyone in town was miserable. The men were physically exhausted from gathering and transporting so many lemons and mentally exhausted from the frustration of never working fast enough to get rid of them all. The women were distraught that they couldn't alleviate their husbands' suffering and despondent that their children would grow up with such an overwhelming obstacle. There was no joy in the town—only sadness. Even Billy's father, the king, once a strong and inspiring sovereign, despaired at the misfortune that had befallen his people. Every day, he would wake up frowning and ask the queen, "Why has this happened to *us*? Why are we so horribly unlucky?" Not knowing what to say, the queen would just nod her head sadly and say, "My darling, I don't know. You're right, it's so awful."

"If only things were *different*," the king would say. "If only all the lemon trees would disappear forever, *then* we would be happy!"

"You're right, darling, we would be so happy with no lemon trees to worry about," the queen would agree.

"Why were *we* given this incredible burden to deal with day in and day out? It has to stop sometime, but when? It seems like we will be stuck under this black cloud for all eternity!" No matter how often the king would ask these questions, every day it was the same: the problem of the lemons grew larger, and there was still no solution. The town was truly lost.

The palace orchard was one of the few places where there were never any lemons; the king employed a growing army of men to keep the place absolutely lemon-free, and he had trained them to catch the lemons before they even hit the ground.

One day, though, as Billy was playing in the orchard, he came across a stray lemon that someone must have dropped by accident. Billy was a very curious little boy, and although he knew that the people in his town considered lemons useless, nothing but a burden, now that he was seeing one right up close, it started him thinking. "Lemons are such a big problem here," he thought to himself, "but what if there's somewhere where lemons *aren't* a problem?" he wondered. "What if someone somewhere knows something that *can* be done with all of these lemons?"

Billy continued to play, lost in his imaginary games, but in the back of his mind, he kept thinking, "There *has* to be something to these lemons beyond what everyone in the kingdom sees." He was sure of it. And that evening at dinner, as he listened to his father and mother complain about the day's lemon numbers, Billy made up his mind: he had to venture outside the kingdom of Lemonville. He had never been outside his father's kingdom before, and he was scared, but he felt something could be done.

Later that night, as Billy was getting ready for bed, his favorite attendant, Jack, noticed that Billy was lost in thought about something.

"What's on your mind, little man?" he asked.

"Lemons."

"Lemons? You don't have to worry about lemons—they will always be cleared out of the way for you. You're the prince, after all."

"But how can I not worry about it? Lemons seem to be slowly killing the kingdom. People are so worried about them all the time that they can't rest, and they're becoming exhausted and sick from the constant work. My father thinks about nothing else all day long. It's scary watching him get sadder and sadder, but he can't find a way out. Even my mother can't make him happy, and she too is becoming sadder and sadder. I was thinking, what if there was something we *could* do with all the lemons that fall?" Billy watched Jack's face for his reaction.

"Something like what?" asked Jack, who knew the boy well enough to let him reach his own conclusions.

"I don't know. But I want to do something so badly. My parents used to tell me that everything happens for a reason, but that was before the lemons became so overwhelming. I don't think they still believe this is true, but maybe it is. Maybe these lemons have been given to us for a reason. Maybe we're too busy trying to get rid of them to see what that reason is. Then again, I don't know. If everyone says lemons are totally useless and nothing but a problem, maybe they're right. Even my parents, who used to say that everything in nature serves a purpose, even *they* say lemons are totally useless." Billy again watched Jack's face for his reaction. His opinion was important to the young boy. "What do you think, Jack?"

"Listen to me," Jack began. "How many people does it take to agree on something before it makes it so? If two people say it's so, does that make it so? If a hundred people say that it's so, does *that* make it so? If the entire kingdom gets together and agrees on something, does *that* make it so?"

"But please tell me what *you* think. Your opinion is important to me!" Billy pleaded.

"Now I think I've said enough. You'll just have to find out for yourself, I guess!"

"But no one agrees with me…what if I'm wrong?" asked Billy.

"Or," said Jack, smiling, "what if you have thought of something for the very first time? What if you discover something new?" he asked. "Now it's time for bed, young man." Jack tucked him in, turned out the lights, and left the boy to sleep.

Billy did not fall asleep quickly that night. He was too anxious and excited in anticipation of the next day; for now, he knew he had no choice but to leave his father's kingdom. He had to go in search of a use for these lemons and a solution to the problem that plagued Lemonville.

Three

Taking the Leap

Prince Billy woke up early the next morning—he had been too excited to sleep very much anyway—and set about preparing for his journey. Since he had never been outside his father's kingdom, he wasn't sure what to take with him, so he filled his knapsack with a few things he thought would be useful. He took a compass that his father had given him, a catapult he had made, and a notebook so he could keep a record of his journey as he went; he also folded in a warm sweater his mother had knit for him and a hunk of bread. He sat down and wrote a short note for his parents. "I'm going to find something really important, I'll be back when I find it." He didn't want his parents to know exactly what he was doing, but he didn't want them to worry about him either. He left the note in the breakfast room where he knew they would see it, slung his knapsack over his shoulder, heaved open the giant iron front door, and stepped out.

The path that led to the palace gates was long and wound around lakes and through forests. It was a beautiful day, and Billy, who loved being outside, had roamed pretty far in the past, so he started out very happily, chasing butterflies and bothering ant-holes as he made his way down the path. But soon he found himself farther from home than he had ever been before, and when he looked back, the palace was little more than a speck in the hazy distance. All of a sudden, Billy was overwhelmed by fear and had to sit down on the ground and hug his knees to stop from trembling. What was he thinking leaving home? He never did things like this; he never struck out on his own. What if he got lost? What if he got cold or hungry? What if he just couldn't do it?

As Billy sat there awash in anxiety and fear of the unknown, he heard the sound of children playing. He was curious—they sounded like they were having a wonderful time. He made his way a little farther down the path and there, around a bend, was a beautiful lagoon with a little waterfall pouring into it. There were five children running and jumping from the top of the waterfall into the clear pool below. Billy did not know these children, and as he watched in curiosity, he noticed that one of the boys seemed afraid to jump—he kept going to the edge and pulling himself back. Soon, all his friends had jumped, and he was standing all alone. Billy watched the boy as he stood peering over the waterfall. Then all of a sudden, after taking a deep breath, he took a running leap over the edge. The next thing Billy knew, the boy was splashing around and laughing with the rest of his friends. He actually seemed to enjoy the water more than anyone else. "I bet he feels proud of himself now that he's jumped," thought Billy.

Before long, the boys noticed Billy sitting and watching them. They decided to see who he was and if he wanted to join in their games. As they climbed up the embankment to where Billy was sitting, he noticed each of them was gnawing on what looked like a big stick. As they approached one of them shouted out, "Hello!"

"Hi," said Billy.

"Want some?" another asked him, holding out his stick, offering the end he hadn't been chewing on.

"What is it?" asked Billy.

"It's a sugar cane. You've never had one?" said the boy who had jumped last.

"No," said Billy.

"It's just something that grows in those fields over there. You can pick it and then you chew it; it's sweet and really yummy. Try it." The boy snapped his sugar cane over his knee and handed a piece to Billy. Billy wasn't sure what to say. His parents had always told him not to accept anything from strangers, but these were children his own age, so he decided there was no harm in accepting their offer and took his half of the stick. The cane was tough, and for a split second, Billy thought they were playing a trick on him, but sure enough, the juice it yielded was delicious.

"Yum," said Billy, smiling. "Thank you."

"Do you want to play with us?" asked the boy.

"I'd love to sometime," said Billy, "but right now, I have to be on my way." He then hesitated. "Do you mind if I ask you a question?" he asked the boy who had been afraid to jump.

"No," the boy said amiably, still very much involved in chewing on his sugar cane.

"I was watching you over there. You were afraid to jump at first, but then you did. How did you stop being afraid?"

The boy shrugged. "I don't know. I had never jumped before, and so I guess I just didn't know what would happen. Then I realized how sad I would feel if I didn't try. So I just did it. It was awesome! I can't wait to go again."

Billy suddenly realized that all it took to get past his own fear was to change his thinking. What *exactly* was he afraid of anyway? "I don't need to worry about getting lost, because I brought my compass," Billy thought to himself. "And I don't need to worry about getting cold or hungry, because I brought a warm sweater and a good supply of food. And that boy probably had a million thoughts like mine about whether he could jump over the waterfall, but he jumped, didn't he? What if I too can do what I'm afraid I can't? Sure I'm scared, but I'm also brave, and I believe that there is something important to gain from my journey, something that no one else has found before." Then it dawned on him: there is no courage without fear.

Billy felt this was a powerful lesson, and he repeated it to himself a few times.

Thanking the boys again, Billy continued down the road, chewing on his delicious new treat. After watching the boy who had been afraid to jump, he realized that if he just changed the way he was thinking, he wouldn't have anything to be afraid of. No longer paralyzed by the doubting voice in his head, he pulled out his notebook and wrote, "There is no courage without fear. The next time I ask myself, 'What if I can't?' I will know the answer: 'But what if I *can*?'"

Four

An Unexpected Blend

Billy had been walking for a few hours and his legs were getting tired, so when he heard a carriage coming from behind him in the distance, he decided to see if he could catch a ride. As the carriage approached, he saw there were two riders, a man and a woman. They appeared to be arguing, but he could not hear what they were saying. As they got closer, Billy could hear that they were arguing about whether or not to stop for him.

"It would be nice to have some company," said the woman, who was rosy cheeked and jolly, with a sweet melodious, laughing voice.

"I don't want some kid back there. He looks like a troublemaker to me," said the man, who was thin and mean looking and spoke with a frown.

By this time, the carriage had reached the spot by the side of the road where Billy was sitting. Still grumbling his reluctance, the man stopped the carriage, while the woman smiled and told Billy to hop on board. "I'm Sweet, and this is my husband, Sour. We're on our way to market." Billy clambered up, thanked the couple for their kindness, and settled into the back of the carriage, nestling between two crates of turnips. "Where are you going young man?" asked Sweet?

"I'm not sure yet," Billy said. "I'm looking for a place where they've found a use for lemons."

"Use for *lemons*?" Sour sputtered. "Everyone knows lemons are nothing but a problem. What a fool's mission!"

Billy grew shy at the man's gruff disapproval, but when he saw Sweet beaming back at him kindly, he spoke up. "Well, I think there might be something we're not seeing, some way of solving the problem that we haven't thought of. I just want to find out for myself."

"That's silly," said Sour.

"Well, I think it's lovely," said Sweet. "You should always follow your heart, and if you believe there's a solution, then you should carry on until you find it."

Billy did not know quite what to say next, so he just thanked her for her words of encouragement and settled back to watch the view as they rolled along.

As they made their way down the road, Billy couldn't help but notice that the couple did nothing but argue and disagree with each other. Sour complained that the carriage was old and falling apart; Sweet countered by saying that it served their needs and was more useful than no carriage at all. Sour started to gripe that this year's harvest was not plentiful enough to support them through the winter; Sweet chimed in to reassure him that they had seen worse harvests in the past and had always gotten along somehow. When he had to stop the carriage for a flock of sheep that was crossing in front of them, Sour fumed at the valuable time they were losing, while Sweet encouraged him to enjoy the sunshine and the beauty around them.

After a while, Billy stopped listening to their conversation and became lost once more in thoughts about his journey. He was now very far from home indeed, and he hadn't thought through exactly *how* he was going to find the place where they had discovered a use for lemons. He watched the fields and trees go by around him, and suddenly he felt like a very small boy in a very big world. "What if Sour was right?" he wondered. "What if lemons really were nothing but a problem? What if his big plan to go out and find a solution just didn't work?"

Billy was roused from his nervous thoughts when they arrived at the market and the carriage came to a clattering halt. Sweet and Sour were still arguing about something, and Billy realized that they had argued the whole way. They hadn't agreed on a single thing. He began to feel rather sorry for Sweet, who seemed so much nicer than her bitter husband. Billy also noticed that she seemed anything but unhappy, and he was suddenly interested in this pair—they were so different from each other, yet they seemed to co-exist so contentedly. Why did they stay together? Why had they married in the first place? It was a puzzle. As they started down from the front of the carriage, Billy sat up and asked if he could help them set up their table. They accepted his offer, and Billy hopped down and tried to figure out how best to lend a hand.

Before he could unload a single crate, he noticed with amazement how quickly and seamlessly the couple set up and displayed their wares. Every time Sour would grunt at the strain of unloading the crates or click his tongue with annoyance as he tried to arrange the vegetables in piles that wouldn't collapse, Sweet would be there to lighten his burden or delicately reposition a cabbage. Almost before he knew it, the stall had been set up and they were arguing over which of them would serve the first customer, who was already approaching. Sour must have won out, because Sweet began to walk towards the carriage, where Billy was still standing looking puzzled, and began to sweep the stalks and leaves that had accumulated during the bumpy ride.

"Well, young man," Sweet said, sweetly, "I suppose you'll want to be on your way now. Not much fun hanging about with a couple of old folks like us. I imagine you'll be wanting to get on with your adventure."

Billy hesitated then decided to ask the question that was now the only thing on his mind. "Sweet, I hope you don't mind me saying, but you seem a lot nicer than your husband."

Sweet's whole body shook with laughter, and she had to stop sweeping and lean against the carriage seat to catch her breath. "Oh, yes dear, everyone says that. He can be a grumpy old codger sometimes, can't he? I wasn't sure when I married him if it would work, what with him and me being so different. But I had a feeling. And don't you think our differences complement each other? He is so sour and gruff that he needs someone sweet and sugary like me to smooth out his rough edges and ease his way through life. On his own, he would scare people off and never sell a single carrot! With me along to soften him up a bit, we do just fine."

Billy thought about this and realized that sometimes things can work even if they seem impossible. Even though this husband and wife seemed like complete opposites, their differences actually helped them get through life together better than they could on their own. While she wants to give away vegetables for free, he likes to keep her balanced and her generosity in check to ensure they make money to live. He thought about his former worries: What if there really was no use for lemons? What if his big plan to save Lemonville just didn't work? Now, after talking to Sweet, he saw that he could answer his own question with an even better one: "What if it does?" He took out his journal and wrote this down so that he would always remember this lesson.

Five

Beyond No

Billy continued on his journey and soon came to a crossroads with two signs pointing in opposite directions. One sign pointed down a road that stretched wide and clear through open fields as far as the eye could see, and said "Scenic route out of Lemonville". The other sign said "Shortcut out of Lemonville" and pointed off the main road down a jagged little path towards what sounded like a fast and furious river, although it was too far for him to see. Billy was unsure of what to do: on the one hand, the safe thing would be to take the wide-open road. But on the other, he knew he wanted to leave the kingdom, so he could not ignore the shortcut sign, even though the road that led in that direction did not look as easy to traverse as the one that stretched out into the flat distance. As he was debating with himself, he heard angry voices approaching from the direction of the river. Soon he could see two men, and even though they were both talking at once, Billy could hear that they were angry about something.

"What an infernal nuisance!" snarled one.

"Village idiot!" spat the other.

"No help at all. We'll have to find another way over the river."

Billy didn't even have a chance to ask them where the narrow road they were coming from led to before they were charging down the main road, still shouting over each other. Soon he heard more voices coming from the direction of the river, getting nearer. This time it was two ladies, and although they were less angry than the first two men had been, they seemed to be talking about the same thing.

"What a strange fool!" exclaimed one.

"Indeed—all he said was, 'No no no.' He must be simple," suggested the other.

Billy jumped at the chance to ask someone what lay down this crooked path.

"Excuse me," he said as politely as he could—he didn't want to startle anyone.

"Hello," they both chimed together.

"I was wondering, what's down there?" he asked, pointing in the direction they had come from.

"A beastly, frightening river and a tiresome idiot who will tell you over and over again that there is no way across, but who will tell you nothing else," said one.

"Don't waste your time," added the other. "He'll tell you the same thing. He told the same thing to those men who came before us. We'll all have to find another way across the river; maybe it's quieter a bit farther along. You can walk with us if you like. Come on."

"Um, actually, no. That's all right, I'm going to stay here for a bit. Thanks, though." Billy knew he wanted to get across the river to get across the mountains, and he was now intrigued by the descriptions of this supposed idiot down by the river—he wanted to check this out for himself.

"Suit yourself," said the first lady. When they turned and made their way down the main road, just as the first two men had done, Billy wondered if he had made the right choice. "What if I can't get across the river to get across mountains at all?" he thought.

"What if 'no' really is the final word?"

But by now, Billy had had enough "what if" thoughts to know that there was always an answer if he just thought about the problem carefully. He decided to try his luck and turned down the river path. His courage and confidence had been building throughout the day. The narrow dirt road was studded with huge rocks and laid over with giant tree roots, so he had to watch where he put his feet, and so he didn't notice the odd-looking little man until he was standing just a few feet away from him.

"Hello!" Billy said, trying to sounds as friendly as possible. The man didn't say anything. Billy looked at the river, which was indeed very fierce looking, then up at the mountains on the other side. He looked back up at the man. Billy wanted to ask the man a different question than the others had put to him, to see if "no" was really all he said. Billy was also getting a bit thirsty, so he mustered up his courage and said, "Excuse me, sir, would you happen to have anything to drink?"

Sure enough, the man just said, "No. No, definitely not. No." But Billy noticed that he was pointing to the river and nodding his head at the same time. Billy thought this was strange indeed, so he asked the same question again, looking up at the man intently. Once again, the man said, "No," still nodding and pointing towards the river, but this time also reaching into some very large pockets and pulling out a steel mug. Billy watched as the man went to the edge of the river, bent down, gathered some water in the mug, and handed it to him. It was cold and bubbling fresh. Billy gulped it down and thought it was by far the coolest, most delicious water he had ever tasted. "Why, thank you," Billy said to this strange man. Since this first request had gone better than expected, Billy decided to go for it and ask how to cross the river.

"Can I cross?" he asked, pointing over at the mountains on the other side.

"No," the man said, almost singing it. "No no no no no." But again, he was nodding his head the whole time.

Billy asked again. "Um, can I cross here?" This time, Billy pointed more emphatically, across the river.

Once again, the man responded, saying, "No" over and over again but continuing to nod yes all the while. Billy decided he had nothing to lose by simply asking him about this strange habit of saying one thing while also saying another. "Uh, sir? Pardon me for asking—why are you saying 'no' but nodding your head as if you mean 'yes'?"

The man suddenly laughed happily. "Do you know you're the first person in *weeks* who's noticed! Most people who come down here looking to cross are so busy staring into the rushing river and coming to their own conclusions that they don't pay proper attention when I answer them, so they only hear me say 'No.' But you, young man, you had an open mind and did not approach me thinking you already knew the answers. For that, you win, and there is a prize."

Billy was pleasantly surprised by the man's animated friendliness, and asked what the prize was.

"You get to cross the river!" he exclaimed. "No is just a word, and there is always something beyond it, even if it's not what you expected. Now, there's a bridge just a little ways down there that will take you easily across the river. Follow me!"

Billy tripped after him, excited and happy that he had come down here to see for himself the funny little man who only said 'no.' He took out his journal and scribbled hurriedly as he followed his new acquaintance: "*NO IS JUST A WORD!* Next time I ask myself, 'What if no is the final answer?' I will remember to ask instead, 'What if it isn't?'"

Six

An End and a Beginning

Billy followed his new friend down the shore a little ways until they came to a bend in the river. As soon as they'd turned the corner, Billy saw a bridge made of logs extending across to the other side. The man put his hand on Billy's shoulder and said, "Cross here, and you will get to where you're supposed to be."

Billy looked at the rickety bridge and the rushing water below and experienced a moment's hesitation. In that moment, many doubts and questions arose in his mind.

"What if I fall in?" he thought. "What if the bridge doesn't hold? What if there are dangerous rocks in the river?" As though reading his mind, the man gave Billy's shoulder a reassuring squeeze and repeated, "Cross here, and you will get to where you're supposed to be." With that, he turned and walked away, soon disappearing back around the bend.

Billy was still a little afraid, but he remembered the boy who had jumped over the waterfall. He also realized that he himself had not gotten this far by letting a little fear hold him back, so he took a deep breath and stepped boldly onto the rickety bridge. When it did not give way beneath him, he was confident enough to take the next step, and the next, and before long he was halfway across.

As Billy continued across the bridge, a strong wind began to blow, causing the bridge to swing and sway. Now seriously frightened, Billy clung to the sides of the bridge for dear life, not knowing whether to go forward or turn back. As he was trying to keep his balance and steady his nerves, a heavy branch from a nearby tree blew by and knocked Billy clear off the bridge. As he plunged into the rushing water and was carried swiftly along by the current, held afloat by his trusty knapsack, he panicked. This was definitely worse than anything that had happened to him so far on his journey. This might have been the worst thing that had happened to him *ever*! Billy was very, very frightened.

Then he remembered the last time he had been afraid, and the words that were written in his notebook. "No courage without fear, no courage without fear…" repeated Billy, as he went rushing along. Calmed and encouraged by these thoughts, Billy started to look around for a way to pull himself out. A short distance down the river, he could see a large rock jutting over the edge of the banks. As he flew by, Billy grabbed onto the rock and pulled himself up and out of the river. Overcome by the effort, Billy collapsed on the grass and fell into a deep sleep.

When Billy awoke, there was a strange-looking old woman peering over him.

"Are you all right?" she asked, seeing that Billy was awake.

"Um…yes…I fell in the river and had to pull myself out. I guess I was tired," said Billy.

"You poor thing!" said the old woman.

"You'll catch cold. Lucky I found you—I'm a medicine woman. You'd better come with me. I'll take you back to my village and we'll fix you right up."

Billy was sniffling and sneezing, so he eagerly accepted the woman's offer, and before long he found himself tucked into a bed in a cabin in the middle of the woods. The old woman had disappeared, and Billy was left alone to think about his situation. He lay there wondering what to do now. He didn't know where he was or where he would go from here. "What if I have to go home now, without having found what I'm looking for?" he thought with dismay. "What if this is the end of my journey?"

When the old woman returned, she had in her hand a small cup, which she handed to Billy.

"Drink this," she said. "It will help you feel better."

"What is it?" asked Billy, sitting up, forcing his disappointment out of his mind.

"It's something healthy and nutritious that I make all the kids here drink. It's packed with vitamins and will speed your recovery," said the old woman.

Billy took a sip and his whole face instantly crumpled—it was the sourest, bitterest thing Billy had ever tasted.

"Oooh, that tastes bad!" said Billy once he had un-crumpled his face. Then, not wishing to appear rude, he asked, "What is it made from?"

"I know it doesn't taste very good, but try to get it down—it really will help you get better. It's lemon juice."

Billy sat up instantly—he could not believe his ears. "Did you say *LEMON?*" he asked, incredulous.

"That's right," said the old woman. "It's full of vitamins and is very healthy, so try to get it down. I'll be back soon to check on you."

She bustled out of the room. As Billy lay there in bed, his mind raced. He'd finally found a place where they used lemons! And although they tasted nasty and sour just as his parents and everyone else had told him, he was so happy to have found that they were healthy and nutritious that he continued to drink the juice, pondering carefully after each nasty sour sip. Now that Billy had solved one problem, he thought maybe there was a way to get beyond the problem of the taste as well. He laughed out loud, remembering the fears he had taken so seriously just moments before. "What if this is the end of my journey?" he had thought to himself then. Now that he had found a use for lemons, and was busy thinking of a way to make them even better, even more useful, he realized this was another important lesson to remember. Billy pulled out his note-book and wrote the following: "You never know what's just around the corner. In the future, instead of asking, 'What if this is the end?' I have to ask myself, 'What if this is just the beginning?'"

Seven

Putting It All Together

As Prince Billy lay sick in bed forcing down his lemon juice, the taste seemed to get worse and worse. Because he had no toys or anything else to do, he took out his notebook. He flipped through the pages, thinking about his journey and re-reading the lessons he'd written down along the way. From the Sugar Cane boys, he had learned that there is no bravery without fear. He would never again let his fear hold him back from trying something new. From his carriage ride to market with Sweet and Sour, he had learned that unexpected elements sometimes blended to make something wonderful. From the Water Man down by the river, he had learned that 'no' is really just a word and that you can always move beyond it to find the 'yes' if you have an open mind. Billy thought about his whole journey and how it had led him to where he was now—in a bed drinking lemon juice…and then all of a sudden he realized…the solution to the problem of the bitter juice was in his notebook—he'd found it along the way!

Billy called for the kindly old medicine woman and asked her for a pitcher of cold water. When she brought it, Billy poured his lemon juice in then took the sugar cane from his bag and stirred it around in the lemony water. The old woman looked on, puzzled. Finally, Billy stopped stirring, poured a little of the mixture back into his cup, and took a sip. The old woman watched Billy's face. Instead of crumpling up from the bitter taste of the juice, it lit up like a spring day!

"THIS IS DELICIOUS!" cried Billy, beside himself with excitement at his new creation. He leapt out of his bed and handed his cup to the old woman. "Taste this!" he said. "Isn't it delicious?" She tasted the cool, sweet liquid and had to agree, it *was* delicious. Prince Billy had taken the sour sting of lemon juice and, by applying all the lessons he had learned, created some-

thing new and wonderful, something delicious and refreshing—he had discovered the solution to all of Lemonville's problems!

"I have to get home!" Billy shouted. "I have to get back to Lemonville and give everyone the recipe!" Billy explained to the medicine woman about his father's kingdom and how unhappy everyone was with all the lemons constantly falling from the trees. "Now we won't have to spend our lives exhausted from clearing away the lemons. Now we can turn them into something that we can all enjoy and benefit from! The kingdom will finally be happy again!" Billy was as excited as a boy can be. The old woman was also beaming.

"Billy, you are a miracle! Not only will this discovery transform the lives of those in your kingdom, but you've made a huge difference for us, too!" she said. "Now we have this delicious drink that we can enjoy all the time! The children will love it, and it will keep us healthy! How can we thank you?" she asked.

Billy thought about his return journey and his excitement at bringing his drink home to share with his parents, Jack, and with all the people in the kingdom. He would have to take enough supplies to make his drink for the whole kingdom. He didn't want anyone to be left out. "That'll mean a lot of sugar cane," he thought to himself. He would need help.

"Well, actually, I could use some help on my way home—I need to gather a lot of sugar cane, and I will definitely need help mixing so much lemonade. Do you think some people from your village could come back with me? I think it would be quicker and more productive if I had a team to work with."

The old woman smiled and said, "You're right, it will be better to work in a team. We're all happy to help you, Billy. I will round up some helpers for you and send you on your way." She gave Billy a pat on the head and left the room.

Billy packed up his things, and before long the old woman was back with a group of about thirty girls, boys, men, and women, all of whom had heard all about Billy's fantastic discovery and were eager to help him on his journey home. Outside, they had prepared a horse-drawn cart to transport the sugar cane that they would gather on the way. Everything was set. Billy thanked the medicine woman for taking care of him and helping him with his discovery, and then he led his new group of friends back to Lemonville.

When they arrived at the gates of Lemonville with their huge cartful of sugar cane, the people who were out clearing the lemons stopped what they were doing and crowded around Billy, relieved for their king that the young prince was home again.

"We must take you to the palace immediately," they urged. "Your parents will be so happy to see you're back safe and sound. They haven't been happy in so many years. Quickly quickly, come come!" They lifted him on their shoulders and started to carry him to the king.

"Wait!" cried Billy. "I have something that will make them even happier, and it will make you very happy too! Put me down; let me show you something before we go to the palace."

Curious, the crowd put him down. Billy directed his new friends to bring the cart to the edge of the waterfall where he had seen the boys jumping on his journey. He then guided them as they tipped the sugar cane over the waterfall and into the clear lagoon below. Then he asked the man with the biggest lemon cart to push it up to the edge and throw the lemons over. The crushed lemons tumbled over the edge and lay in the lagoon, bobbing and glinting in the sun. Billy raced down to the water, cupped his hands, and drank from the pool. It was the same sweet, delicious drink he had made before, only now there was enough for everyone in Lemonville to taste, and Billy beckoned for them to do so. "Come taste it. Come taste the *lemonade!*" The word just flew out of his mouth.

"What did you call it?" asked a grumpy old man, who was glad that the prince was home but now wanted to get back to hauling lemons.

"Lemonade…I don't know…it just popped out! But that's what I think we should call it…now drink!"

"Why, I'll be darned! This is the most refreshing and delicious thing I've tasted in years!" exclaimed the grumpy old man, no longer so grumpy. Billy put some lemonade in a bottle and led the way to the palace.

When Billy got home the king and queen hugged Billy so hard that they almost spilled all the lemonade. With tears in their eyes, they rejoiced that he was home and safe.

"Where did you go? What were you looking for?"

"Mom, Dad, I didn't know exactly what I was looking for, but I found it. I think you'll like it. Actually, I think you'll love it." He handed the bottle of lemonade to his father, and then his mother, and watched as they tasted and smiled.

"But I've never tasted anything so delicious.…" His father took another sip. "What is it?" he asked his son.

"I've decided to call it lemonade. It's the solution to our problems here in Lemonville! It's lemon juice mixed with sugar cane and water. Isn't it yummy?" Billy was so excited that his dad seemed to like it. He felt enormous pride at having helped, and he also felt enormous joy that his father's kingdom would no longer be under a black cloud.

"But how on earth did you come up with this?" asked the king. "We must go tell your mother at once!"

As the pair made their way through the palace to find the queen, Billy told his father all about his journey. He told about how he had been afraid at first but had learned about being brave and trying new things. He told about the funny couple who argued but lived so happily and how they had taught him that sometimes you can mix two completely different things and create something amazing. He told about the strange man who only said "no" and how he had learned that no is often just a station stop on the way to yes. He told about the kind old medicine woman who had given him the sour-tasting juice, and how he had put everything he had learned together to create this wonderful new drink.

"But what made you go searching in the first place?" asked the king. "What made you think there was anything more to lemons than trouble and bother?"

"I just saw it differently," said Billy. The king was humbled by his young son's explanation, at once so simple and so wise. Not only was the king grateful to his son for saving the kingdom, but he was also enormously proud and vowed then and there to learn from his son's positive way of looking at the world.

The very next day, the king issued a proclamation. The whole kingdom heard about what the young prince had done and got to taste lemonade for the first time. From that day forward, the Kingdom of Lemonville was a happy one, filled with joy and laughter.

Now they are very glad to have so many lemon trees; the children play and swing from their branches while their mothers and fathers look on, grateful that their lives are no longer over-shadowed by lemons. And all because Prince Billy taught them how to turn the lemons that fall into the sweetest lemonade.

Eight

Billy's Lemon-Aid Stand

Billy's mother finished her story and looked down at her son, expecting him to have drifted off. She was surprised to see him looking up at her, wide eyed and smiling.

"Did you like that story?" she asked him, reaching to push his hair out of his eyes.

"Very much," he said, quietly.

"Tired?" she asked?

"A little," he said, yawning. "Can I ask you a couple of things about the story?"

"In the morning you can ask me all you want, okay, sweetie? We'll talk about it at breakfast. Let's go to sleep now—it's late. Goodnight, baby. See you in the morning. Big day tomorrow." She leaned over and kissed him on the forehead and then left him to sleep, pulling the door closed softly after her.

Billy fell asleep wondering what the story meant, and that night he dreamt of lemons falling over waterfalls into sugary lagoons; in the morning, for the first time since his dad had passed away, he woke up excited to get out of bed. He ran downstairs, where his mother was already fixing one of her traditional weekend breakfasts: pancakes, eggs, and bacon—all Billy's favorites. He poured himself some juice and sat down at the kitchen table.

"Mom, what did that story mean?" he asked.

His mother smiled at her son's eager inquisitiveness. She piled a couple of pancakes on to a plate and set it down in front of him. "What do *you* think it means?" she asked, getting some pancakes and sitting down herself. Billy thought for a minute.

"I think it means that sometimes bad things happen, but that if you want to you can change the bad things into okay things—maybe even really good things."

Billy's mother smiled. "That's pretty much exactly right," she said. "You know, Dad dying…"

She paused. "Dad dying is a really, really sad thing. It's totally okay to be sad, to miss him. I miss him terribly, but…but.…" She paused again.

"But if you stop seeing it as *just* something sad, you can turn it into whatever you want," Billy chimed in.

"Absolutely right," said his mother.

"There's no way to know what's going to happen. We never know what's going to be put in our path for us to deal with. In Lemonville, they had to deal with lemons, and in our life we have to deal with losing Daddy. But just as the prince saw beyond what everyone else saw, we can choose to see something more in losing daddy. If you just change the way you look at something, the thing you're looking at changes. Prince Billy saw the lemons differently—he challenged himself to move beyond his fear and his doubt, beyond other people's common conclusions, beyond where others had become complacent, past what *looked* like a problem—and look what he did! He turned this huge problem into a great opportunity and saved the kingdom!"

"Yeah…" Billy said, looking solemn.

"Even if you don't see it right now," Billy's mother continued, "there *is* a way to turn your father's death into something that will help you, and others, *if* you're like Billy the Prince— which I think you are, very much indeed."

Billy smiled, and that was the last they spoke of the Prince of Lemonville. For the rest of breakfast, they talked about Billy's lemonade stand. After breakfast, Billy got straight to work. He got the picnic tables out of the garage, dragged them down to the end of the driveway, and covered them with tablecloths. He just had one thing left to do. He had to make his sign. Billy sat and thought about the prince. He thought about how he had kept pushing himself further and further, past every problem he encountered on his journey. He felt lucky to know the story of how lemonade was invented, and he wanted to be like the prince, always making the most and best out of everything.

And then Billy realized he *was* like the prince. He was taking lemonade and transforming it into something truly wonderful: a way of helping children who didn't have enough to eat. "I'm turning lemonade into lemon-*aid*!" he said to himself, excited. Then he realized what he should write on his sign; he took the biggest sheet of paper he could find, and in bright red marker wrote in gigantic letters:

BUY MY LEMON-AID
FEED THE WORLD ONE CHILD AT A TIME

He hung it on a tree at the end of the driveway. It looked great. Billy ran to bring his mother out to see it, and he wished his dad could be there to see it too.

Finally, ten o'clock rolled around, and it was opening time. Billy lugged a couple of cold pitchers of lemonade out to the tables and sat patiently waiting for his first customer. It was only a few minutes before kids from the neighborhood started trickling past; by noon, there was a constant stream of people from all over town lining up to buy his lemon-aid. With each quarter that dropped into his collections tin, Billy thought of the prince. He felt so lucky to know that there is *always* a way to turn lemons into lemon-aid.

About the Authors

Joshua A. Shaw is a recognized business leader across a number of industries. He was a self-made millionaire by the ripe age of twenty-four, and at age thirty, he has already built three successful companies.

After building and selling his first company and taking his second one public, he is now building his third venture, GoSMILE.

He has quickly become a driving force in the cosmetics and beauty industry, as the co-founder and chief operating officer of GoSMILE, Inc. In less than three years, he and his amazing partners have established GoSMILE as the innovative pioneer and leader of the newest category of Prestige Specialty business, called Smile Beauty™. Building the company from its nascent stages in mid-2002 to the mid size high-performance company it has become in the industry over the past three years, Josh has demonstrated his knowledge and expertise in developing, launching, and managing successful organizations.

Prior to GoSMILE, he successfully helped build and run a multimedia marketing services company, Student Advantage Inc., valued at over a billion dollars in the stock market at its peak. Over a nine-year period, Josh built and managed various aspects of the business, including marketing, operations, sales, and business development. He played an integral role in the successful evolution of the business from start-up to public entity, driving the growth of the company from twelve people generating $400k in annual revenue to nearly five hundred people generating over $85MM in annual revenue.

Josh's philanthropic work includes Autism Speaks, Operation Smile, and Ronald McDonald House. He received his BS in Marketing and Finance from State University of New York, Albany, and lives in New York City with his wife Melissa, where they make lemonade together every day.

Alexandra L. Barzvi, Ph.D. is a Clinical Psychologist. Dr. Barzvi is also the Clinical Director of the Institute for Anxiety and Mood Disorders at the New York University Child Study Center. She is an expert in Cognitive Behavioral Therapy and specializes in working with children, adolescents and families. Dr. Barzvi's areas of expertise include Anxiety, Depression, Parenting, and Family Relationship Enhancement. She speaks nationally and provides training workshops, consultations and seminars for mental health professionals, school personnel and parents. She is a member of the Association for Behavioral and Cognitive Therapy and the Anxiety Disorders Association of America.

Dr. Barzvi's philanthropic work includes her role as managing editor of HEART Magazine, a not-for-profit magazine that provides a voice for people, organizations and events devoted to making a positive difference in the world today. She is also the founder of TogetherWorks.org, an organization devoted to creating opportuni-

ties for individuals to join together as a community dedicated to service.

The power of
positive
perspective...

And What about Autism Speaks?

It was 4 PM on a Tuesday afternoon during the final *Apprentice* task when I met Alison Singer, senior vice president of Autism Speaks. Interested at first by the charity, I listened carefully as she explained the mission of Autism Speaks. I had never heard of autism beyond the movie *Rain Man*.

I was immediately blown away by the staggering statistics:

- Ten years ago, 1 in 10,000 children was diagnosed with autism. Today, that number if 1 in 166.
- Sixty-seven children are diagnosed per day, a new case is diagnosed almost every twenty minutes.
- More children will be diagnosed with autism this year than with AIDS, diabetes, and cancer combined.

- Autism is the fastest-growing serious developmental disability in the United States.

As she continued, I found myself more and more startled by the stories she told about her personal experience as the mother of young daughter with autism. Her description of the relentless challenges faced by families struggling with this disorder was overwhelming and heart-breaking.

As a person who is passionate about family and communication, I was shocked at the magnitude of this debilitating disorder. Imagine this could happen to a child—your friend's or even your own. Speechless? Lost? Suffering from uncontrollable tantrums? Unable to make friends? This just could not be.

The fact that many children with autism can't speak, share feelings, or express simple emotions was inconceivable to me. How was this possible? What was being done about it? And why had the number of children affected by autism risen to such staggering levels over the last ten years? I started to realize just how silent this disease was.

Autism Speaks seeks to bring a voice to that silence. It promotes awareness, raises money, and funds the scientists who search for answers. It helps families navigate an agonizing journey. It brings hope to a community of heartbreak.

The final words Alison spoke that day will remain with me for a long time: "I only hope that one day my daughter will look at me and say, 'Mommy, I love you.'" That moment, I became committed to helping Autism Speaks raise awareness, fund research, promote early detection, and ultimately find a solution for this frightening disorder affecting so many people around the world.

You see, we are all dealt lemons in life—large and small. In some cases, those lemons are a failing grade in a class, a broken leg, a broken relationship, or even the discovery that your child has a disease like autism. However, it is completely within our ability to accept the lemons we have been dealt and make lemonade. It all depends on the power of positive perspective.

I salute Autism Speaks for bringing a voice to a community in dire need of one, and for helping the parents, friends, teachers, and families of those combating autism make lemonade on their lifelong journey.

In partnership, Autism Speaks and NYU Child Center will help bring a voice to autism.

Smiles for the Cure

I would also like to take this opportunity to thank my amazing partners at GoSMILE.

They embody the passion, spirit, and vision found in only the greatest leaders in the world. They are smart, inspiring, and caring people with an acute appreciation for life.

In support of the mission to bring a voice to Autism Speaks, GoSMILE has developed a special-edition toothpaste called GoSMILE Lemonade Smile. A portion of the proceeds will benefit Autism Speaks.

This product exemplifies the passion within our company as well as our greater interest: we not only want to sell amazing products, but also want to have an amazing impact on the world in the process.

Thank you all for being who you are.

www.GoSMILE.com

978-0-595-37861-6
0-595-37861-7

CPSIA information can be obtained at www.ICGtesting.com
Printed in the USA
LVOW062137270911

248170LV00002B/202/A